Chicano Calligraphy Workbook For Beginners

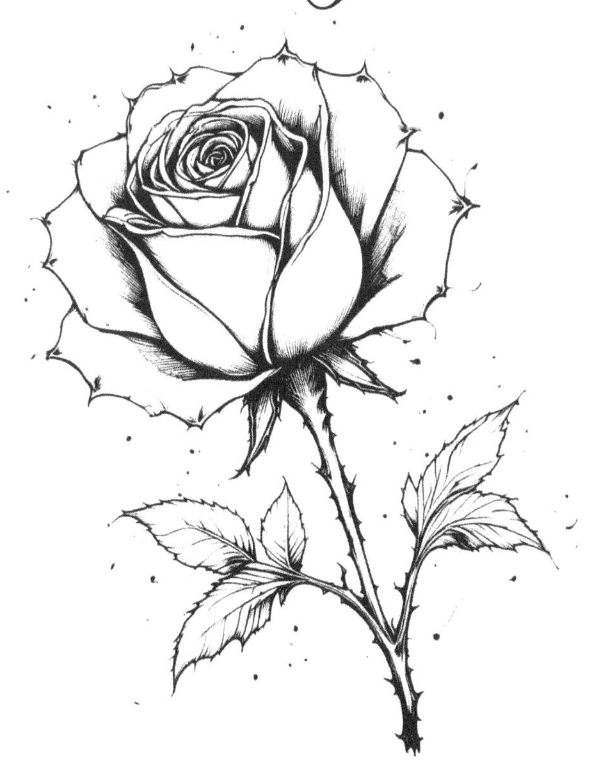

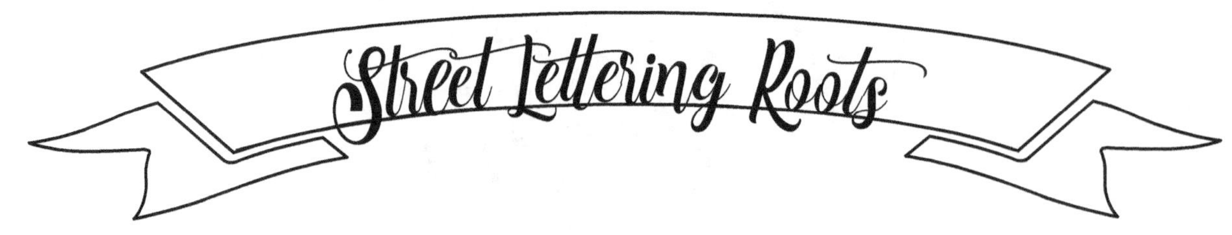

LET'S KEEP IT REAL—CHICANO CALLIGRAPHY AIN'T ABOUT RULES OR PERFECTION. IT'S ABOUT SOUL, ATTITUDE, AND REPPIN' WHERE YOU COME FROM. YOU DON'T NEED A ROYAL SCRIPT TO SHOW PRIDE— YOU NEED FLOW, CONFIDENCE, AND A STEADY HAND.

GET YOUR POSTURE RIGHT. GET THAT PEN TIGHT. THIS STYLE'S ALL ABOUT BOLD MOVES AND CLEAN LINES WITH FLAVOR. LET YOUR INK TALK.

Movement

SIT SOLID, FEET PLANTED, ELBOW LOOSE. LET YOUR ARM GLIDE LIKE A LOWRIDER DOWN THE BOULEVARD—SMOOTH, STEADY, INTENTIONAL. THIS AIN'T FINGER-WORK, IT'S FULL-BODY RHYTHM. YOU AIN'T DRAWING LETTERS, YOU'RE DANCING WITH THEM.

Tool of the Trade

YOUR PEN IS YOUR VOICE. WHETHER IT'S A SHARPIE, BRUSH PEN, OR OLD-SCHOOL CHISEL TIP—HOLD IT LIKE YOU MEAN IT. TILT IT, GRIP IT, FIND THAT ANGLE THAT FEELS LIKE YOU. THE FIRST LINES MIGHT SHAKE—BUT THAT'S JUST PART OF YOUR ORIGIN STORY.

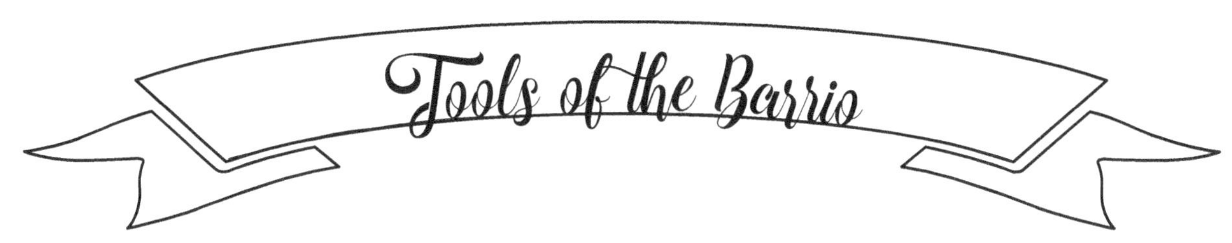

YOU DON'T NEED A FANCY ART SHOP TO START—REAL ONES BEGIN WITH WHAT THEY'VE GOT. THAT BEING SAID, IF YOU'RE LOOKING TO LEVEL UP YOUR STYLE, HERE'S WHAT THE HOMIES USE:

★ PENCILS

PERFECT FOR SKETCHING YOUR FLOW BEFORE COMMITTING WITH INK. KEEP IT LOOSE, LIGHT, AND FULL OF ATTITUDE.

★ PENS

FINELINERS, GEL PENS, OR BALLPOINTS—IF IT GLIDES SMOOTH, IT'S FAIR GAME. GO BOLD OR GO HOME.

★ BRUSH PENS

THESE BEASTS GIVE YOU THICK-N-THIN STROKES IN ONE FLICK. START WITH SOMETHING FIRM FOR CONTROL—THEN UNLEASH YOUR WRIST LIKE YOU'RE TAGGING A WALL AT NIGHT.

★ SHARPIES & MARKERS

CLASSIC. RELIABLE. LOUD. THESE WILL GIVE YOUR CHICANO LETTERING THAT RAW, STREETWISE EDGE.!

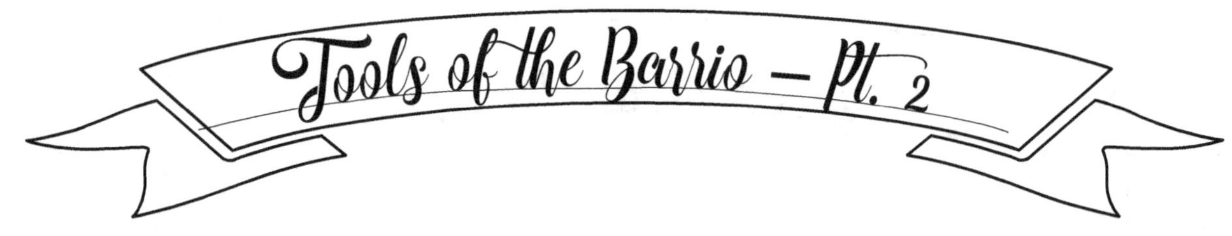

YOU ALREADY KNOW—EL ESTILO CHICANO DOESN'T NEED A MOUNTAIN OF FANCY GEAR. JUST GIVE US A SMOOTH PEN, SOLID PAPER, AND CORAZON. STILL, HERE ARE SOME WEAPONS OF CHOICE YOU MIGHT WANNA MESS WITH:

★ CHALK

CHALK MARKERS HIT DIFFERENT. WITH A LITTLE FLOW AND FIRME STROKES, YOU'LL BE ROCKIN' CHALKBOARD SIGNS, MURALS, AND SIDEWALK ART THAT MAKE PEOPLE STOP AND STARE. CHALK CALLIGRAPHY'S GOT THAT STREET VIBE, PURO CORAZON.

★ PAPER

PAPER AIN'T JUST PAPER, ESE. GO WITH THE THICK STUFF—LIKE CARDSTOCK—TO KEEP YOUR LINES CLEAN AND AVOID BLEED-THROUGH. THIN PAPER'S WEAK AND KILLS YOUR MOJO. YOU WANT YOUR PEN TO GLIDE LIKE LOWRIDER WHEELS ON SUNDAY.

★ FUDENOSUKE PEN

THESE FINE BOYS ARE TIGHT FOR CRISP, THIN LINES. PERFECT IF YOU'RE GOIN' FOR CLEAN LETTERING BEFORE HITTING BOLD STROKES. FUDENOSUKE IS LIKE THAT STEADY HOMIE—ALWAYS SHOWS UP, ALWAYS SMOOTH.

★ BRUSHES

BRUSH PENS? MAN, THEY'RE YOUR RIDE-OR-DIE FOR BIG, BOLD LETRA STYLE. WANNA ADD ROSAS OR FILIGREE? THESE BAD BOYS GOT YOU. GREAT FOR FREESTYLE PIECES AND DETAIL THAT MAKES YOUR PAGE POP.

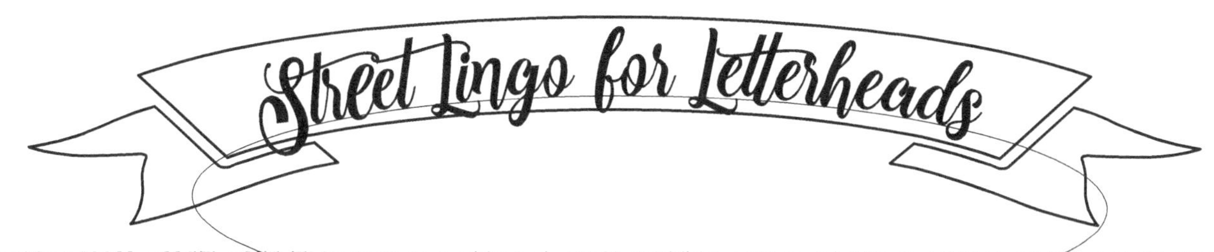

BEFORE YOU BUST OUT THE BOLD LETRAS, YOU GOTTA KNOW THE BASICS. THIS AIN'T SCHOOL, HOMIE—IT'S MORE LIKE LEARNING THE CODE OF THE CALLE. GET THESE TERMS DOWN, AND YOUR LETTER GAME GONNA HIT HARDER.

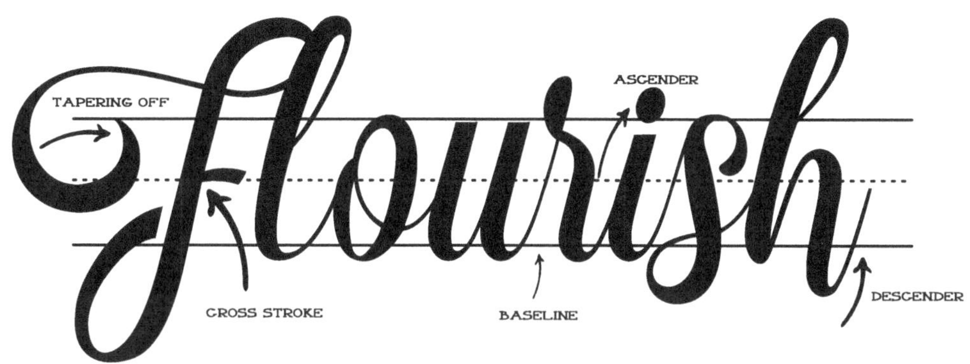

★ DESCENDING STROKE

DOWNWARD PRESSURE—THIS STROKE ADDS WEIGHT. LIKE PUTTING YOUR FOOT DOWN IN A TAG. HEAVY AND BOLD.

★ ASCENDING STROKE

UPWARD FLOW—LIGHT AND CLEAN. LIKE THAT FIRST LIFT BEFORE YOU HIT THE CURVE.

★ ASCENDER

THE TOP PART OF A TALL LETTER. LIKE THE HOOD OF A T OR H. STRETCHES UP WITH PRIDE.

★ DESCENDER

THE PART THAT DROPS LOW—LIKE THE TAIL OF G OR Y. LOWRIDER STROKE, SMOOTH AND STYLIN'.

★ FLOW

THAT RHYTHM IN YOUR LETTERS, ESE. SMOOTH LIKE A FREESTYLE RAP. MAKES YOUR WORDS DANCE.

★ CROSSBAR

HORIZONTAL HIT—LIKE IN F, T, OR H. STRONG LIKE A BRIDGE.

★ LETTERFORM

THE FULL SHAPE OF YOUR LETTER—YOUR LETRA'S ID, ITS VIBE, ITS SIGNATURE.

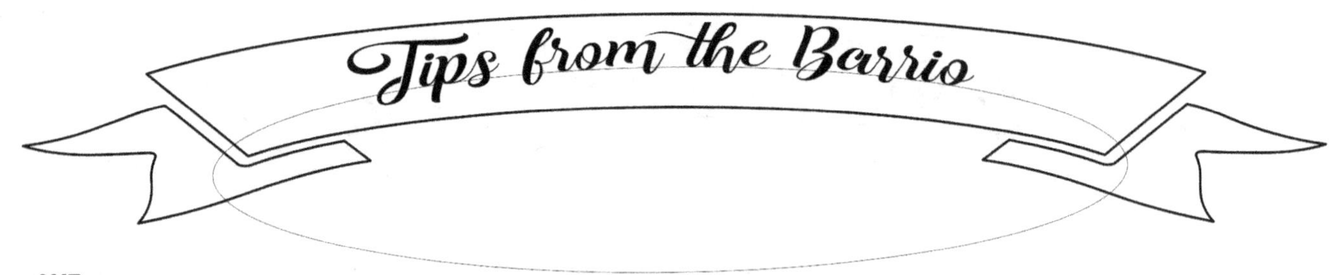

- ONE

TAKE YOUR TIME, HOMIE. EACH LETTER IS A PIECE OF ARTE. DON'T RUSH IT LIKE YOU'RE SCRIBBLIN' A NOTE—TREAT IT LIKE A MURAL WITH SOUL..

- TWO

START WITH A PENCIL—ES TU MEJOR AMIGO. SKETCH IT RAW, ERASE THE MESS, AND SHAPE YOUR FLOW 'TIL IT HITS JUST RIGHT.

- THREE

LIFT THAT PEN AFTER EACH STROKE. THIS AIN'T CURSIVE, VATO. CHICANO STYLE IS STEP BY STEP—CONTROLLED, FIRME, AND SHARP.

- FOUR

GOLDEN RULE? DOWNSTROKES HIT HARDER. THICKER = POWER. THAT CONTRAST? THAT'S YOUR SIGNATURE MOVE.

- FIVE

UPSTROKES? KEEP 'EM LIGHT LIKE A WHISPER. LET YOUR HAND FLOAT IN AND OUT, SUAVECITO.

- SIX

PRACTICE IS THE REAL OG. NAIL EACH LETTER SOLO, THEN START STRINGIN' THEM TOGETHER. PLAY WITH LAYOUT, ADD YOUR OWN FLOURISHES (LA FIRMA), AND LET YOUR STYLE SPEAK.

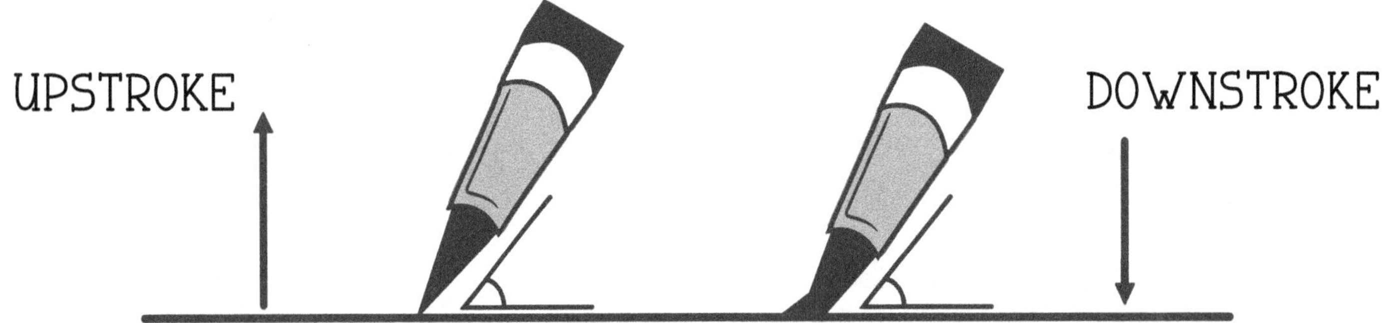

GET YOUR PENCILS, MARKERS, WHATEVER YOU GOT—'CAUSE NOW WE'RE GOIN' IN DEEP. THIS IS WHERE YOUR CHICANO LETTERING JOURNEY REALLY BEGINS.

Basic Strokes
BARRIO STYLE

THIS IS HOW YOU BUILD YOUR FLOW, ONE STROKE AT A TIME. FAUX CALLIGRAPHY'S LIKE THE SKETCH PHASE—NO PRESSURE TRICKS, JUST CLEAN LINES AND FULL CONTROL. PERFECT IF YOU'RE ROLLIN' WITH A PENCIL OR FINE-TIP MARKER.

NO FANCY FLICKS HERE YET—THIS IS ABOUT DISCIPLINE. ABOUT GETTING EACH STROKE FIRME BEFORE YOU START THROWIN' ATTITUDE ON THE PAGE.

GRAB YOUR LAPIZ, PRIMO. VAMOS A ESCRIBIR CON ESTILO.

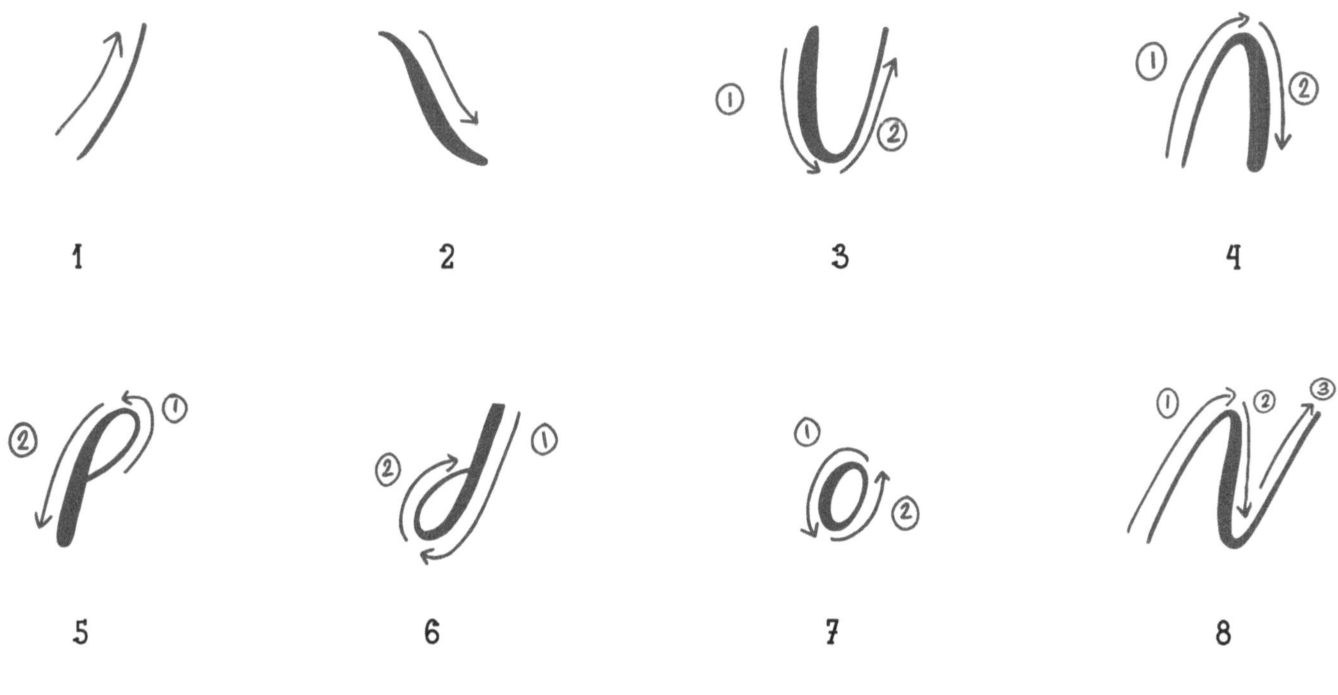

1. HIGH STROKE
2. LOW STROKE
3. BACKSTROKE
4. REVERSE STROKE
5. ASCENDING LOOP
6. DESCENDING LOOP
7. OVAL
8. COMPOUND CURVE

Upward Vibe

- START LOW AND GLIDE UP LIKE YOU'RE CATCHIN' A BREEZE.

- KEEP IT LIGHT, FIRME, AND TIGHT—LIKE THAT FIRST MOVE IN A TAG.

- NO RUSH—YOUR STROKE SHOULD RISE LIKE SMOKE, THIN AND ELEGANT.

Power Strokes

- FROM THE TOP DOWN, HOMIE. BRING THE PRESSURE LIKE YOU MEAN IT.

- START CLEAN, GET BOLD. THIS STROKE IS ALL ABOUT FUERZA AND FLOW.

- EASE UP AT THE END TO LET IT FADE SMOOTH—JUST LIKE THE TAIL OF A LOWRIDER TURN.

The Climb

- THINK OF THIS STROKE LIKE YOU'RE RISIN'—SLOW, STEADY, PROUD.

- LIGHT PRESSURE, FIRME CONTROL. LET YOUR HAND GLIDE LIKE A RHYTHM.

- KEEP IT CONSISTENT LIKE A PRAYER CANDLE BURNIN' ALL NIGHT.

El Giro

- START SOFT, THEN SWITCH IT UP—LET YOUR STROKE FLIP AND DROP WITH STYLE.

- THAT CLEAN BLEND FROM UP TO DOWN? THAT'S YOUR SIGNATURE SPIN, ESE.

- PRACTICE UNTIL YOUR TURNAROUND LOOKS SMOOTHER THAN A MIDNIGHT CRUISE.

Ascending Loop

Descending Loop

Oval

Compression of Turns

BOLD, FLOWING & FIERCE – LETRA GRANDE CON ESTILO

EVERY UPPERCASE LETTER HERE IS YOUR FOUNDATION. THINK BLOCK MEETS BARRIO—STRONG, PROUD, FULL OF FLAVOR. START SLOW. STAY FIRME. YOUR FLOW WILL COME, LETRA POR LETRA.

Mi Estilo Practice Page

THIS IS YOUR PAGE, HOMIE. MAKE IT YOURS.

STRONG LINES, SMOOTH CURVES – LETRA GRANDE PARTE DOS

THESE LETRAS ARE LIKE BLOCK SOLDIERS—EACH ONE WITH ITS OWN VIBE. GET YOUR WRIST LOOSE, YOUR LINE CLEAN, AND LET YOUR PEN WALK TALL.

H

I

J

K

L

M

N

Freehand Barrio Practice

LETRA FUERTE. LETRA VIVA. THIS IS YOUR IDENTITY, BRO.

Chicano Lettering — Uppercase Style O—U

CURVES, CUTS & CALLE — LETRA GRANDE PARTE TRES

SOME LETRAS TWIST. SOME STAND TALL. THESE ONES GOT SWAGGER. BRING OUT THE FLOW, KEEP IT FIRME, AND DON'T BE AFRAID TO EXAGGERATE THAT SPIN.

BarrioFlow Practice Page

STYLE AIN'T TAUGHT—IT'S TRAINED. KEEP GOIN', ESE.

Chicano Lettering — Uppercase Style V–Z

SHARP CUTS & BARRIO RHYTHM – LETRA GRANDE FINAL

THESE LAST LETRAS HIT HEAVY—BOLD, RAW, AND FULL OF FLOW. THE X MARKS TERRITORY. THE Y STRETCHES DOWN LIKE A SHADOW. AND Z? THAT'S THE FINAL FLICK. END YOUR SET LIKE A SIGNATURE TAG: FIRME AND UNFORGETTABLE.

Practice Page — Let's Keep the Flow Going

YOUR FLOW'S JUST WARMING UP—TIME TO HIT THOSE LOWERCASE MOVES, FIRME Y SUAVE.

Chicano Lettering — Lowercase Style a—g

SMALL LETTERS, BIG FLOW — LETRA PEQUENA PARTE UNO

LOWERCASE MIGHT BE SMALL, BUT IT BRINGS SERIOUS PERSONALITY. THESE LETRAS CURVE, FLICK AND DIP—EACH ONE'S GOT ITS OWN BARRIO BOUNCE.

a a a a a a a a a a a

b b b b b b b b b b b b

c c c c c c c c c c c c c

d d d d d d d d d d d

e e e e e e e e e e e e e e

f f f f f f f f f f f f f f

g g g g g g g g g g g g

Flow Practice — Letras Pequeñas

KEEP YOUR WRIST LOOSE, HOMIE—THIS IS WHERE THE STYLE GETS SPICY

Chicano Lettering — Lowercase Style h—n

STREET CURVES & SMOOTH CUTS — LETRA PEQUENA PARTE DOS

THESE MID-SET LETRAS GOT MOVEMENT—BOUNCE, HEIGHT, ATTITUDE. STAY LIGHT ON THE UPSTROKES, FIRME ON THE DOWN. LET YOUR HAND GROOVE WITH EACH FLICK.

h

i

j

k

l

m

n

Keep That Flow Rolling — Practice Page

STAY SMOOTH, VATO—THESE ARE THE LETTERS THAT HOLD THE WHOLE WORD UP.

Chicano Lettering — Lowercase Style o—u

LETRA PEQUENA PARTE TRES – ROUND FORMS, TIGHT FLICKS

THESE LETRAS ARE ALL ABOUT CURVES Y CONTROL. LET YOUR PEN MOVE LIKE SMOKE—SOFT, FIRME, AND WITH RHYTHM. KEEP YOUR FLICK TIGHT, AND LET THOSE O'S ROLL LIKE LOWRIDER RIMS

o

p

q

r

s

T

u

Practice Your Flow — O to U

KEEP THAT WRIST STEADY, ESE. YOU'RE BUILDING LETTERS WITH SOUL.

Chicano Lettering — Lowercase Style v–z

LETRA PEQUENA PARTE CUATRO – FINAL FLOW FORMS

LAST LETRAS, BUT NO LESS FIRME. THESE ONES ARE SHARP, SLICK, AND FULL OF FINAL FLAIR. THAT Z? THINK OF IT AS THE FINISHING SLASH ON YOUR NAME—BOLD AND UNSTOPPABLE.

Wrap Up the Lowercase Flow

YOU HIT EVERY LETRA. NOW GET READY TO MIX 'EM LIKE A REAL STREET WRITER.

Chicano Lettering — Street Numbers 0–6

BOLD, CLEAN, BARRIO STRONG

NUMBERS SPEAK TOO, HOMIE. WHETHER IT'S YOUR BARRIO CODE, BIRTH YEAR OR STREET REP, MAKE THOSE DIGITS FIRME. KEEP IT CLEAN. KEEP IT TIGHT. LET EVERY STROKE TALK WITH PRIDE.

0 0 0 0 0 0 0 0 0

1 1 1 1 1 1 1 1 1 1 1

2 2 2 2 2 2 2 2 2 2

3 3 3 3 3 3 3 3 3 3 3

4 4 4 4 4 4 4 4 4

5 5 5 5 5 5 5 5 5 5 5

6 6 6 6 6 6 6 6 6 6 6

Practice Page — Digits en Estilo

NUMBERS WITH FLOW. WRITE 'EM LIKE THEY MEAN SOMETHING.

Chicano Lettering — Street Numbers 7—9

SECOND SET – ROUND OUT THE BARRIO CODE

THESE FINAL DIGITS SEAL THE DEAL. THAT 7 CUTS SHARP, THE 8 GOT FLOW, AND 9 DROPS WITH HEAVY SWING. WHEN YOU WRITE NUMBERS, WRITE THEM LIKE THEY REP SOMETHING REAL—YOUR TIME, YOUR PEOPLE, YOUR TRUTH.

7 7 7 7 7 7 7 7 7 7 7

8 8 8 8 8 8 8 8 8 8 8 8

9 9 9 9 9 9 9 9 9 9

Practice Page — Code It With Style

YOU GOT THE DIGITS—NOW STACK THEM WITH MEANING.

Chicano Script – Estilo Elegante

THIS VARIATION BRINGS A SMOOTHER, MORE REFINED TOUCH TO YOUR LETTERS. PERFECT FOR NAMES, DEDICATIONS, POEMS – OR ANYTIME YOU WANNA ADD A LITTLE CLASS TO YOUR STREET FLOW.

Practice Page — Estilo Elegante

EVEN THE BARRIO GOT ITS GRACEFUL MOVES, HOMIE.

Chicano Script — Estilo Elegante

THIS SET'S ALL ABOUT CONTROL. THESE LETRAS GLIDE—LONG, LEAN AND FULL OF FLOW. KEEP 'EM CLEAN, FIRME, AND SHARP LIKE A FRESH CUT.

Practice Page — Barrio Grace

STYLE AIN'T ALWAYS BOLD. SOMETIMES IT WHISPERS SMOOTH.

Chicano Script — Estilo Elegante

BIG CURVES, BOLD STANCE — THESE LETTERS DON'T WHISPER. THEY SHOW UP LIKE
THEY OWN THE BLOCK. MAKE EVERY STROKE SPEAK YOUR TRUTH.

Practice Page — Stroke With Pride

WHEN YOU DRAW THESE, PICTURE 'EM ON A WALL, 3 METERS WIDE.

Chicano Script — Estilo Elegante

THESE FINAL STROKES CUT CLEAN. THEY'RE ANGULAR, FAST, FULL OF ATTITUDE —
LINE A SIGNATURE THAT DOESN'T ASK FOR PERMISSION.

Practice Page — Show Your Signature Style

THAT Z? THAT'S NOT JUST A LETTER. THAT'S YOUR DROP-THE-MIC STROKE

Lowercase Script — Estilo Elegante

THESE SMALL LETTERS DON'T SHOUT—THEY GLIDE.

WORK THAT WRIST, LET YOUR HAND DANCE, AND GIVE EACH LOOP SOME FLAVOR.

a a a a a a a a a a a

b b b b b b b b b b b

c c c c c c c c c

d d d d d d d d d d

e e e e e e e e e

f f f f f f f f f f f f f f f f f f f f f f

g g g g g g g g g g g g g g g g g

Practice Page — Flow & Precision

YOUR FINESSE SHOWS IN THE SMALL STROKES. KEEP IT FIRME, KEEP IT CLEAN.

Lowercase Script — Estilo Elegante

FROM THE TALL REACH OF H TO THE BOUNCE OF M—
THESE STROKES ARE YOUR RHYTHM SECTION. KEEP THAT BEAT STEADY.

h

i

j

k

l

m

n

Practice Page — Bounce & Flow

LETTERFORMS LIKE M & N TEST YOUR BOUNCE CONTROL—MASTER THEM AND THE REST WILL FOLLOW.

Lowercase Script — Barrio Flow

THESE LETRAS LEAN SLICK AND LOW — THINK SMOOTH STROKES WITH STREET SOUL.

KEEP YOUR WRIST CHILL, LET THE TIP GLIDE.

Practice Page — Flow with Control

EVEN THE SMALLEST LETTERS GOTTA HIT HARD — EVERY CURVE, EVERY FLICK TELLS A STORY.

Small Letters —Firme & Finessed

SMOOTH LIKE BARRIO WHISPERS, EVERY LETRA GOT ITS OWN FLAVOR. STAY STEADY, STAY CLEAN.

Practice Sheet – Tu Estilo in Motion

EVERY STROKE YOU DROP? THAT'S YOUR NAME ECHOING LOUD – FIRME Y REAL.

Chicano Lettering — Street Numbers 0—6

THESE DIGITS GOT CURVES WITH ATTITUDE. IT AIN'T JUST MATH — IT'S MUSCLE MEMORY AND RESPECT. KEEP IT FIRME, KEEP IT CLEAN, LIKE EVERY NUMBER'S GUARDING YOUR NAME.

Your Turn — Rep Your Digits

RESPECT EACH LINE. EVERY REP BUILDS YOUR REP.

Chicano Lettering — Street Numbers 7–9

THESE LAST DIGITS? PURE EDGE. CURVES AND CUTS THAT SLICE THROUGH PAPER LIKE CHROME ON ASPHALT. INK WITH INTENT—LIKE YOU'RE FINISHING YOUR BLOCK TAG WITH PRIDE.

Finish Strong — Your Street Flow

DON'T SLOW DOWN NOW. YOUR STYLE'S ALMOST LOCKED IN.

Chicano Lettering — Barrio Phrases Vol. 1

THESE AIN'T JUST WORDS. THEY'RE THE ONES YOU'D WRITE ON A WALL, IN A NOTEBOOK, OR ACROSS YOUR NAME. LET THEM GLIDE OFF YOUR HAND WITH SWAGGER AND MEANING.

Mi Vida Loca

Stay True   Stay True

Trust No One

La Familia   La Familia

Ride or Die   Ride or Die

Respect All Fear None

Born to Hustle Born to Hustle

Trace it like ink flows from your soul.

THESE AIN'T JUST WORDS. THEY'RE THE ONES YOU'D WRITE ON A WALL, IN A NOTEBOOK, OR ACROSS YOUR NAME. LET THEM GLIDE OFF YOUR HAND WITH SWAGGER AND MEANING.

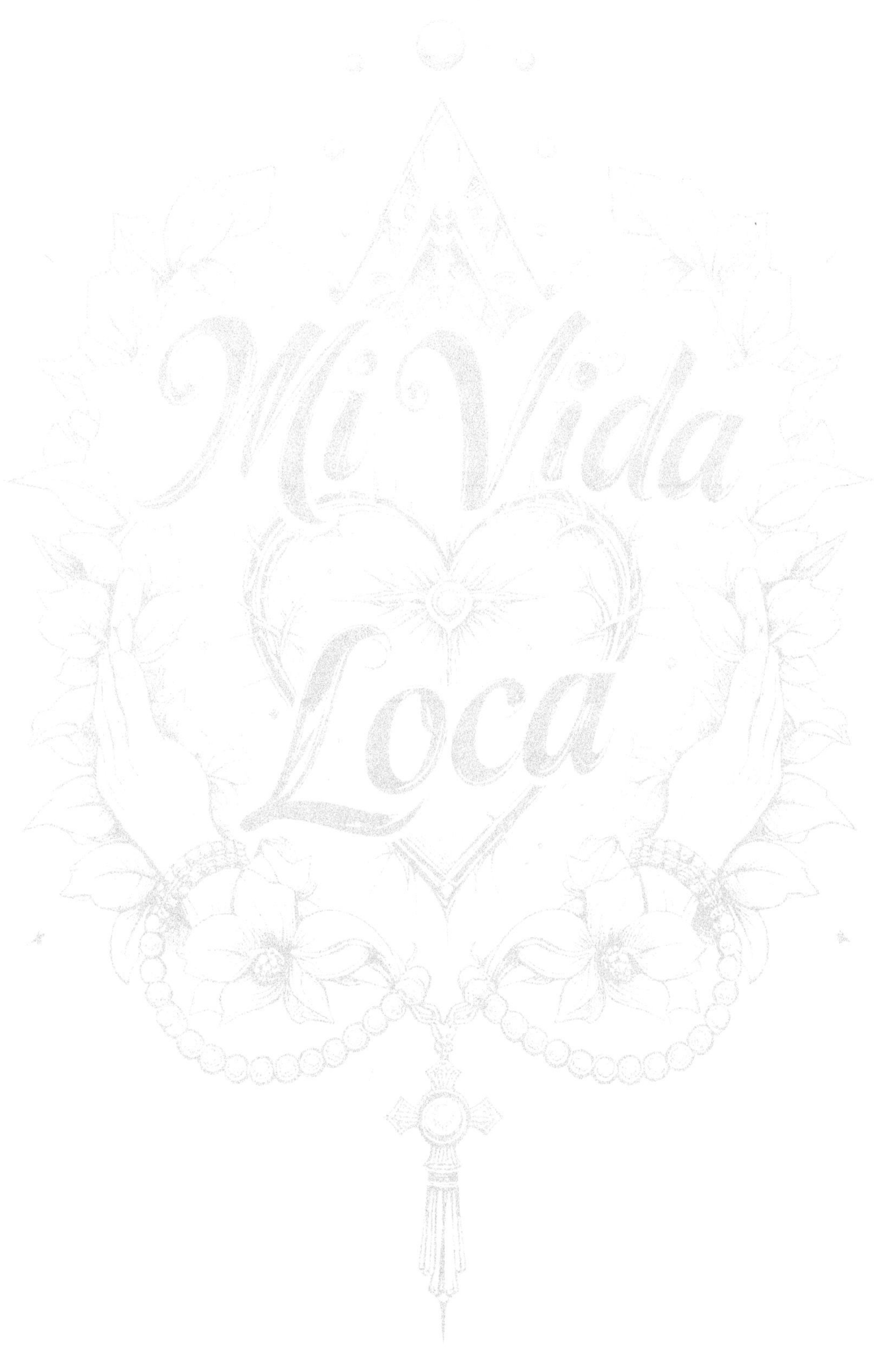

Chicano Lettering — Street Sayings, Set 1

SAY IT LOUD. SAY IT FIRME

Stay Strong Stay Strong

Familia First

No Regrets No Regrets

Ride or Die Ride or Die

Pure Heart Pure Heart

Barrio Love Barrio Love

Sin Miedo Sin Miedo

Ink Tracing Page — Stay Strong

RACE THE ARTWORK BELOW WITH FOCUS AND FLOW. LET EACH LINE TEACH YOU CONTROL. THIS ISN'T JUST TRACING — IT'S TRAINING YOUR HAND TO MOVE WITH MEANING.

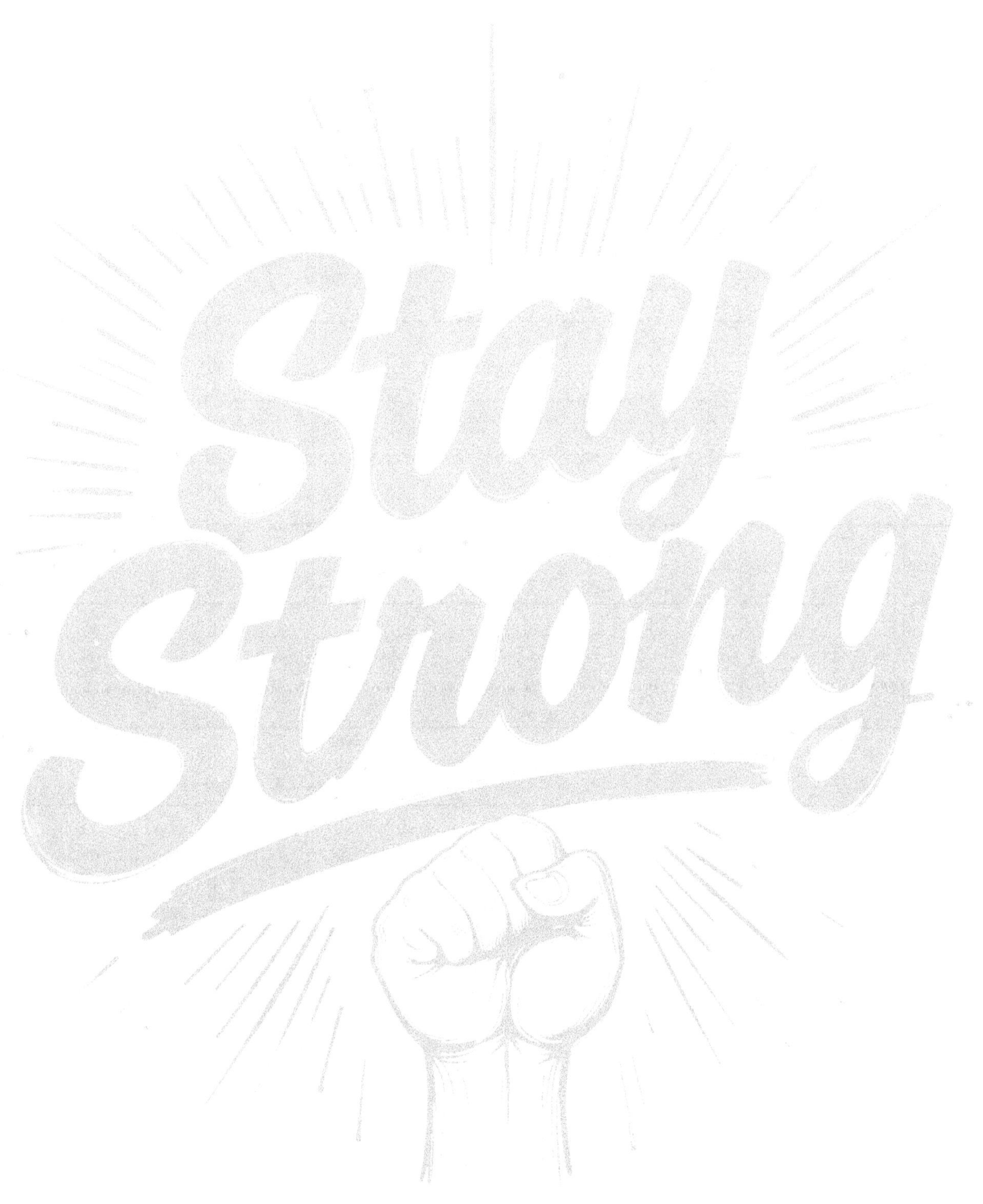

Chicano Lettering — Street Sayings, Set 2

SEVEN PHRASES, ONE MESSAGE: KEEP IT REAL.

Loyalty Over Everything

Forgive Nothing

Street Raised Street Raised

Smile Now Cry Later

Hustle Hard Hustle Hard

God Knows My Heart

One Life One Chance

Ink Tracing Page — Loyalty Over Everything

FOLLOW EVERY LINE WITH INTENTION.

TRACE BOLD. TRACE CLEAN. LET YOUR LOYALTY FLOW THROUGH YOUR STROKES.

Chicano Lettering — Street Sayings, Set 3

INK THE MESSAGE. LET THE STROKE SPEAK

Fear Nothing Fear Nothing

Love Runs Deep

My Roots My Rules

Made in the Streets

Trust Few Trust Few

Strength Within

Real Ones Only

Ink Tracing Page —Fear Nothing

STEADY YOUR HAND. LET THE STRENGTH IN EACH STROKE REMIND YOU: FEAR NOTHING

CALM HAND, LOUD MESSAGE.

One Love One Life

Rise Above

Stay Silent

Corazón de Oro

Built From Pain

Always Watchin'

Nothing But Respect

Ink Tracing Page — Built From Pain

TRACE LIKE YOU'VE BEEN THROUGH IT. EVERY LETTER'S A SCAR TURNED INTO STYLE.

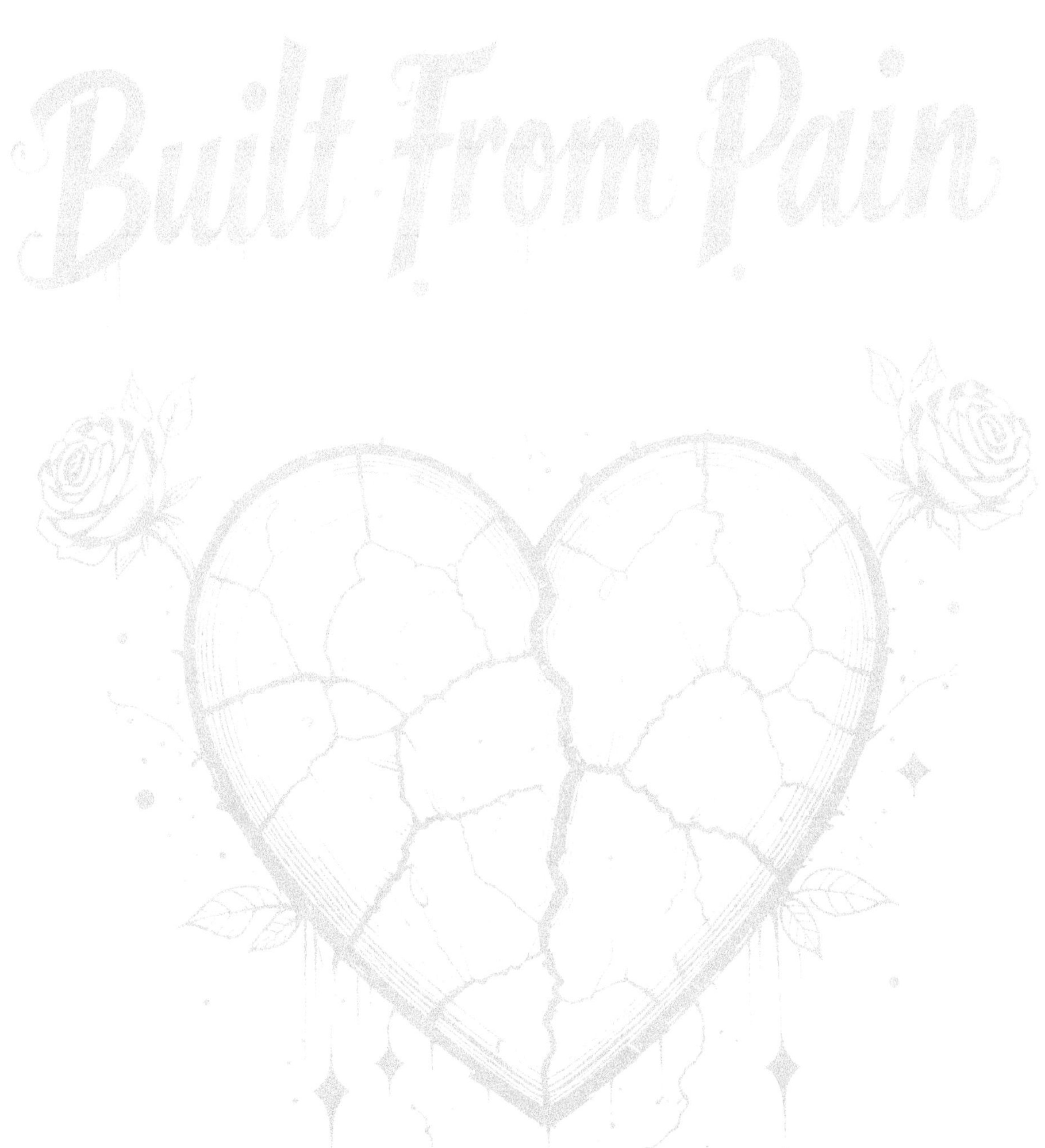

INK YOUR SPIRIT. EVERY STROKE IS PRAYER AND POWER.

Faith Over Fear

Pray for Strength

Eyes on the Light

Never Alone

Blessed & Battle-Tested

Trust the Process

Forgiven Not Forgotten

Ink Tracing Page — Faith Over Fear

STEADY HANDS. CLEAR FOCUS. LET YOUR FAITH FLOW IN EVERY STROKE YOU TRACE.

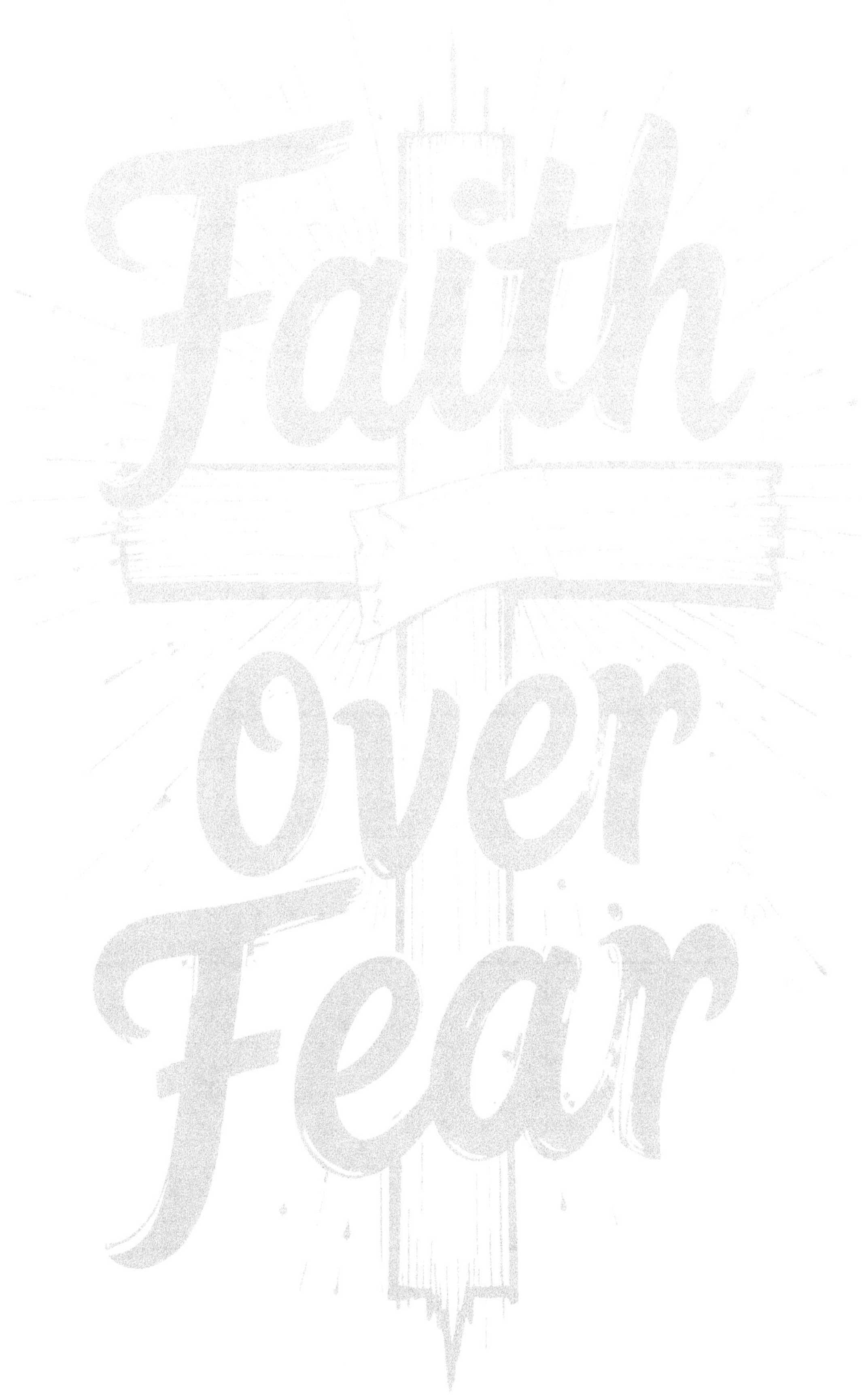

Chicano Lettering — Street Sayings, Set 6

Earned Not Given

Lessons Hurt

Real Over Perfect

Hard Times Built Me

Pain is Fue

Roots Run Deep

Nothing to Prove

Ink Tracing Page — Hard Times Built Me

TRACE EACH LETTER LIKE YOU'VE LIVED EVERY WORD. STRENGTH COMES LINE BY LINE.

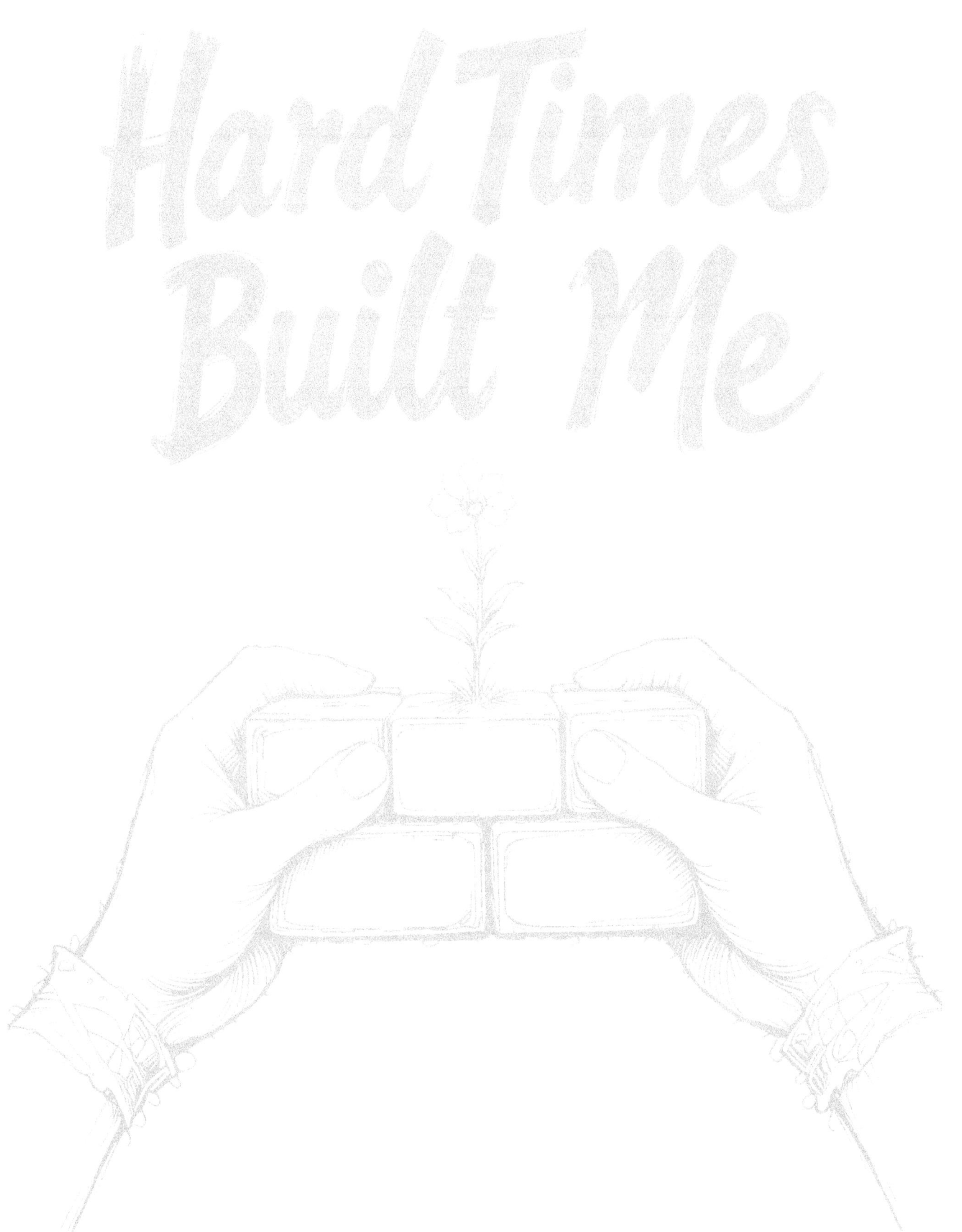

Chicano Lettering — Street Sayings, Set 7

LOYALTY. SILENCE. REAL ONES DON'T TALK — THEY WRITE.

Day Ones Only

Respect Is Earned

My Silence Speaks

Loyal by Nature

Still Standing

Brotherhood Runs Deep

Speak in Silence

Ink Tracing Page — My Silence Speaks

TRACE WITH FOCUS. THIS PIECE DON'T SHOUT — IT WHISPERS STRONG.

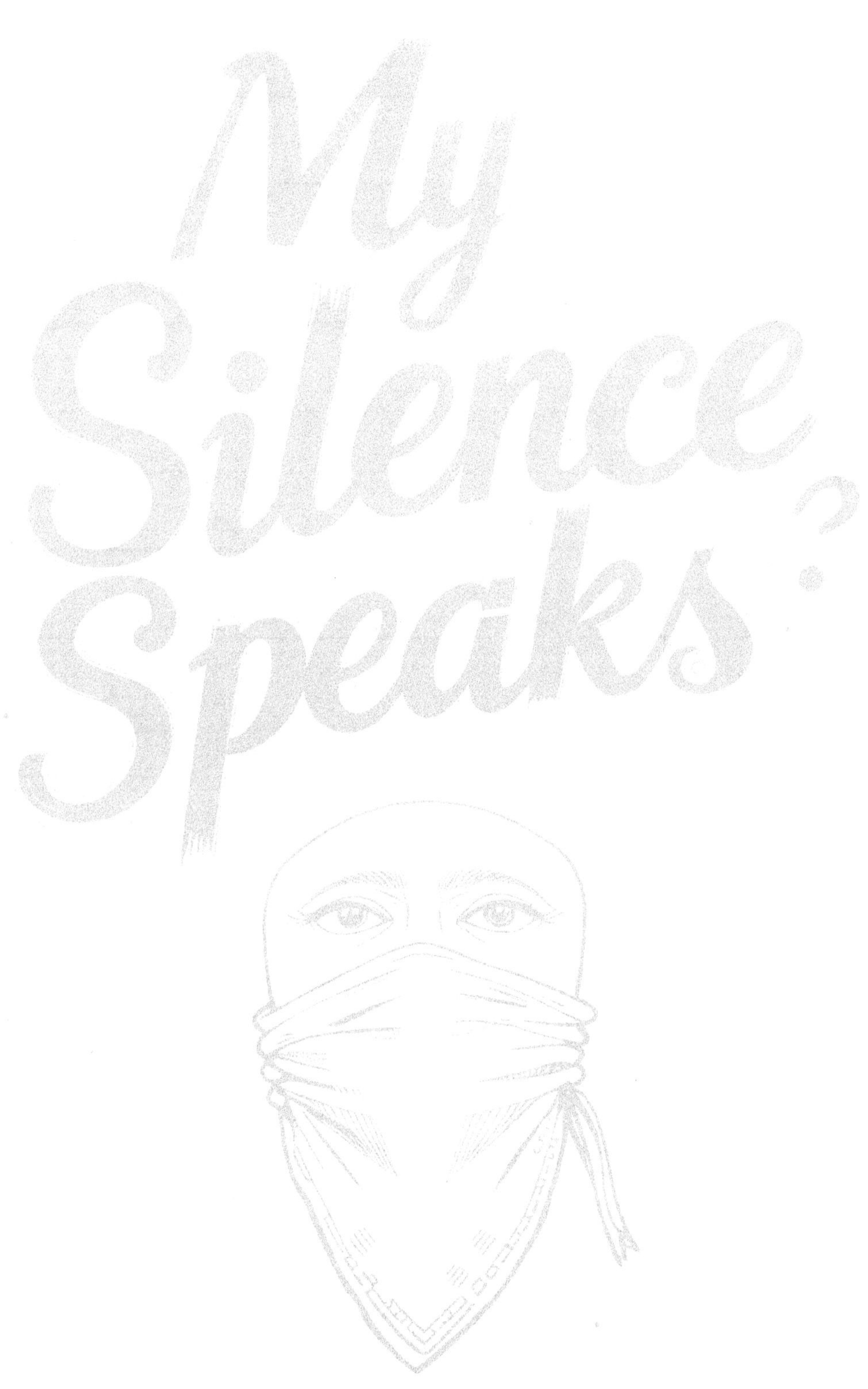

KNOW YOUR WORTH. INK YOUR TRUTH.

Born from Struggle

I Am My Story

Never Fold

Mind on a Mission

Raised with Pride

Silent Strength

Silence Is Power

Ink Tracing Page — NeverFold

TRACE IT SOLID. YOUR STROKES SHOULD STAND TALL, JUST LIKE YOU.

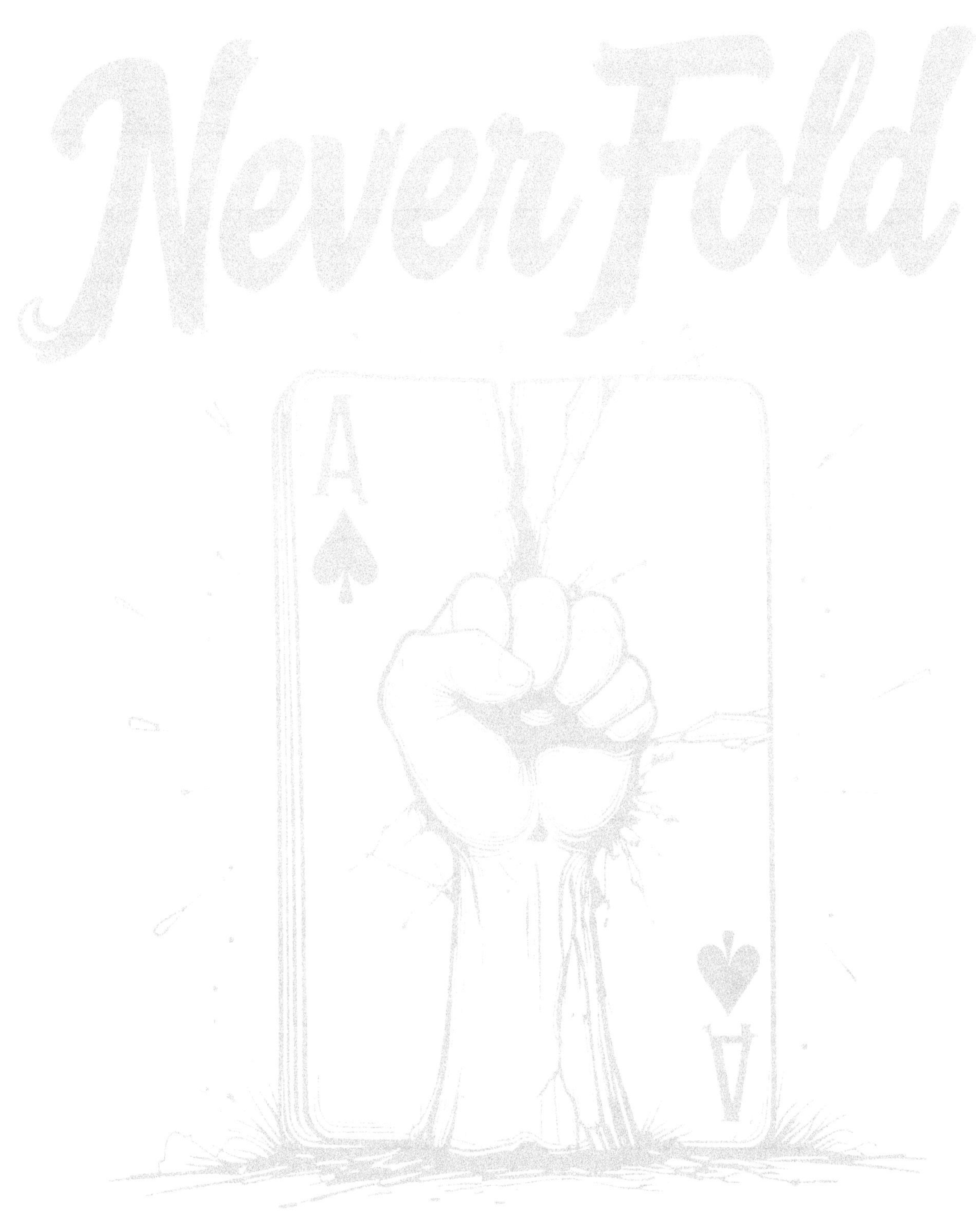

PRESSURE BUILDS DIAMONDS. SO DO THESE LETTERS.

Write your world

Embrace every letter

Lines create magic

Grace in script

Ink your vision

Words as art

Create timeless art

Ink Tracing Page — Fall Seven Rise Eight

TRACE EACH LETTER LIKE A COMEBACK. FALL, RISE, WRITE, REPEAT.

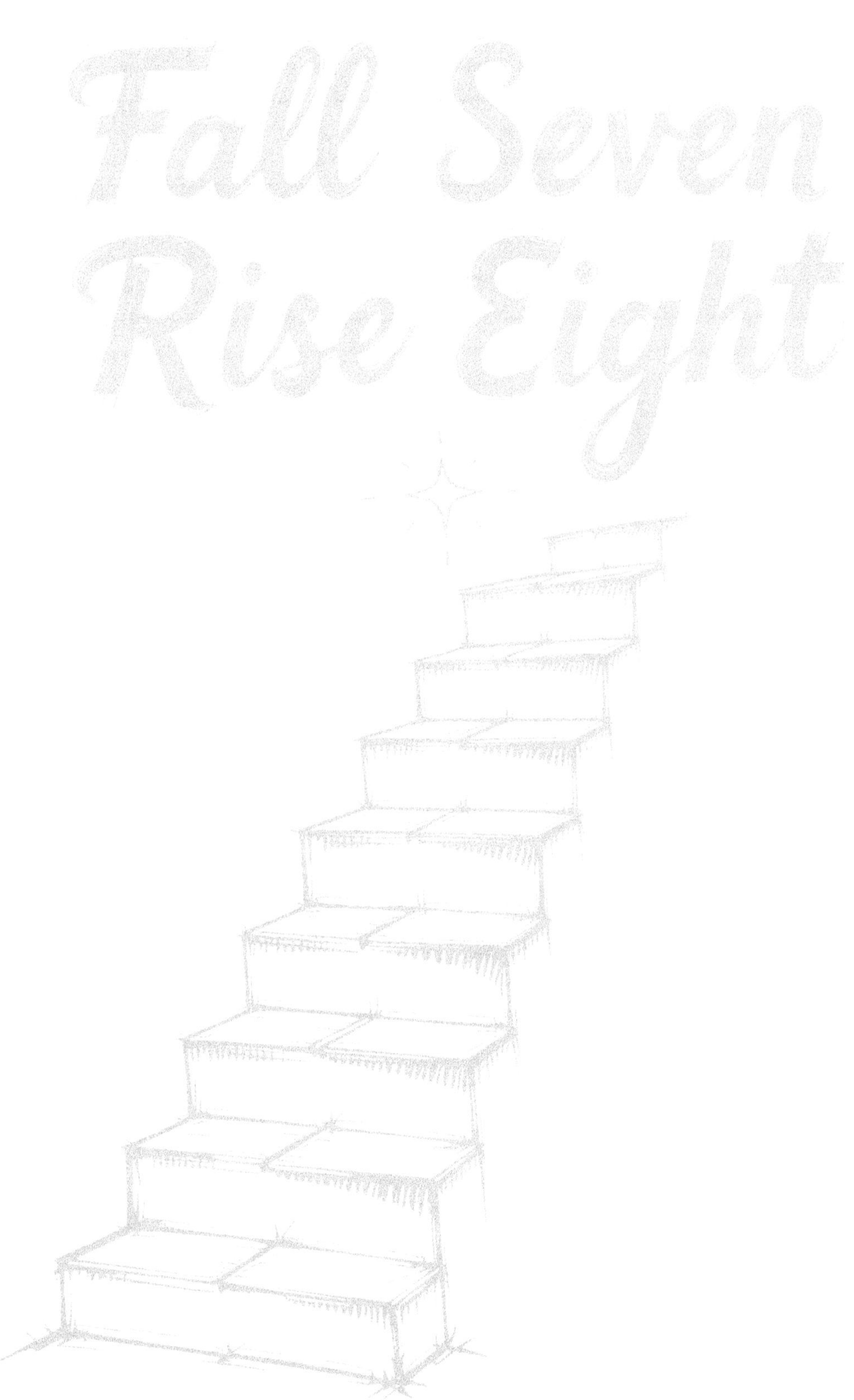

LET THE LAST STROKES SPEAK FOR WHO YOU ARE.

Ink Runs Deep

Written in Blood

The Streets Remember

Always Been Me

Legacy Over Hype

Words Hold Weight

Built to Last

Ink Tracing Page — Legacy Over Hype

THIS ONE'S NOT FOR FLASH. IT'S FOR THOSE WHO LEAVE SOMETHING BEHIND.

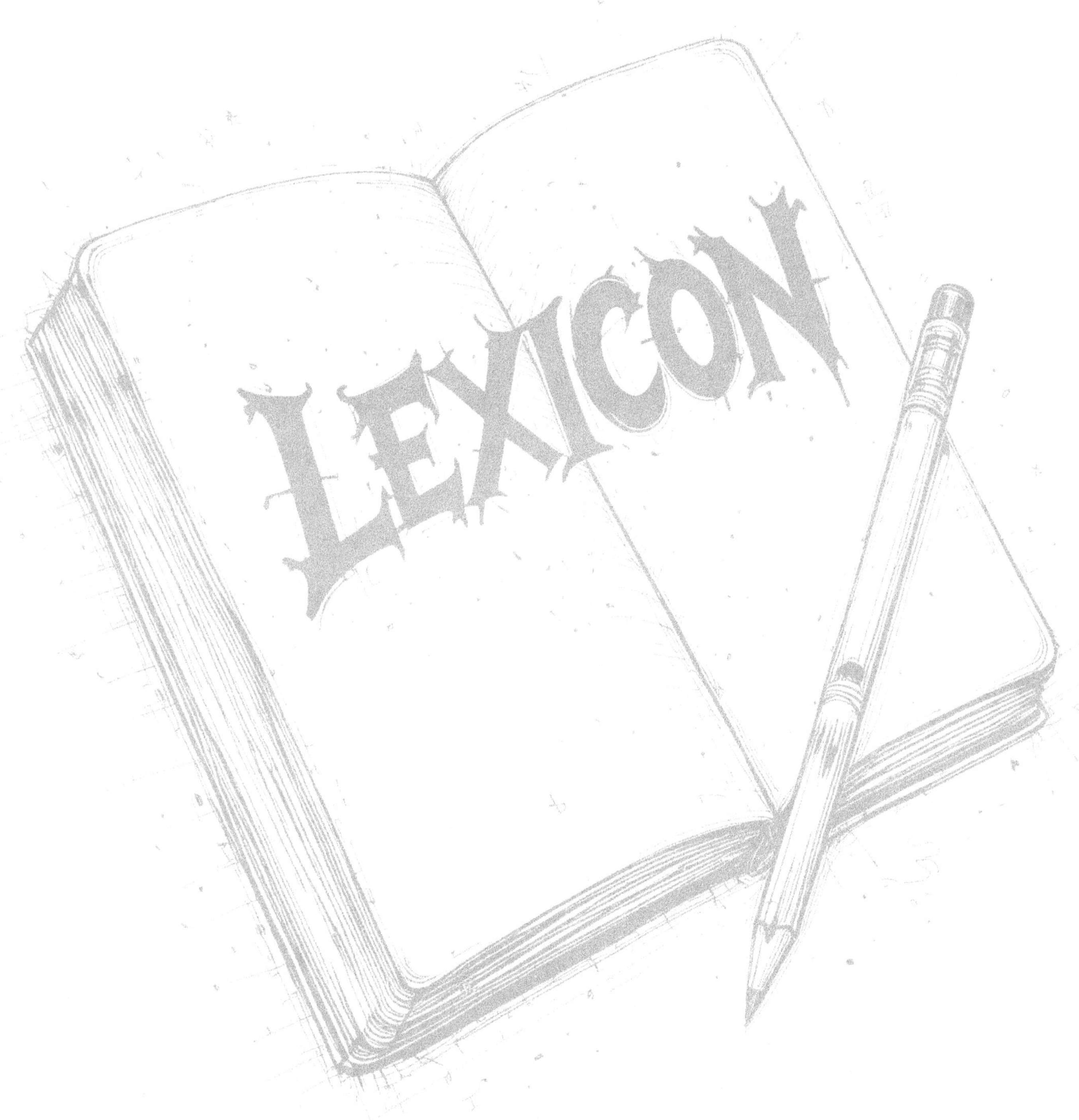

LEXICON

Barrio Lettering Lexicon

WORDS WITH MEANING. INK WITH ROOTS

STREET LANGUAGE. CALLIGRAPHY SOUL.

FIRME – SOMETHING CLEAN, SOLID, STYLISH. HIGH PRAISE IN THE BARRIO.

MI GENTE – MY PEOPLE, MY COMMUNITY. THE ONES YOU RIDE WITH.

PLACA – A TAG OR NAME WRITTEN IN GRAFFITI OR STYLIZED CALLIGRAPHY.

LETRAS – LETTERS. THE SHAPE OF YOUR MESSAGE.

BARRIO – NEIGHBORHOOD. NOT JUST A PLACE, BUT WHERE YOUR ROOTS RUN DEEP.

LA RAZA – THE PEOPLE. CULTURAL PRIDE AND UNITY IN CHICANO IDENTITY.

LOCO / LOCA – CRAZY. FEARLESS, EMOTIONAL, WILD WITH SOUL.

CHICANO STYLE – BOLD, PROUD, RAW. A MIX OF IDENTITY, ART, AND DEFIANCE.

HOMIE – A CLOSE FRIEND OR BROTHER. MORE THAN A BUDDY.

TAG – A PERSONAL SIGNATURE, WRITTEN WITH STYLE AND ATTITUDE.

RESPETO – RESPECT. YOU DON'T ASK FOR IT – YOU EARN IT.

CARNAL – A BROTHER BY BLOOD, OR SOMEONE JUST AS CLOSE.

ORALE – "RIGHT ON," "HELL YEAH," "LET'S GO" – ENERGY IN ONE WORD.

SIMON – "YES." CONFIRMATION WITH STREET FLAVOR.

CHALE – "NO WAY." "FORGET THAT." DISBELIEF OR PUSHBACK.

ESE – CLASSIC TERM FOR A GUY OR HOMIE. OLD SCHOOL.

JEFITA / JEFITO – MOM / DAD. LOVING AND RESPECTFUL TERMS.

TRECE / 13 – SYMBOLIC NUMBER TIED TO IDENTITY AND STREET PRESENCE.

RANFLA – CAR, USUALLY A LOWRIDER. THE RIDE THAT TELLS YOUR STORY.

LOWRIDER – ROLLING ART. CULTURE ON WHEELS.

CALLE – THE STREET. NOT JUST PAVEMENT – HISTORY, PAIN, PRIDE.

GACHO – BAD, MESSED UP, WRONG. SOMETHING TO CALL OUT.

VATO / VATO LOCO – DUDE. CRAZY DUDE. WILD, LOYAL, REAL.

HEINA – YOUR GIRL. A ROMANTIC OR RESPECTFUL TERM FOR A WOMAN.

BARRIO QUEEN – A STRONG WOMAN FROM THE NEIGHBORHOOD. RESPECTED.

CLIKA – YOUR CREW. HOMIES WITH LOYALTY.

TRUCHA – STAY SHARP. KEEP YOUR EYES OPEN.

TINTA – INK. FOR TATTOOS OR CALLIGRAPHY – THE SAME SOUL.

ROLL CALL – SHOUT-OUT TO YOUR PEOPLE. REPRESENTING WHO'S HERE.

OG – ORIGINAL GANGSTER. RESPECTED, SOLID, BEEN THERE.

RESPECT THE INK – HONOR THE ART, THE PROCESS, THE MESSAGE.

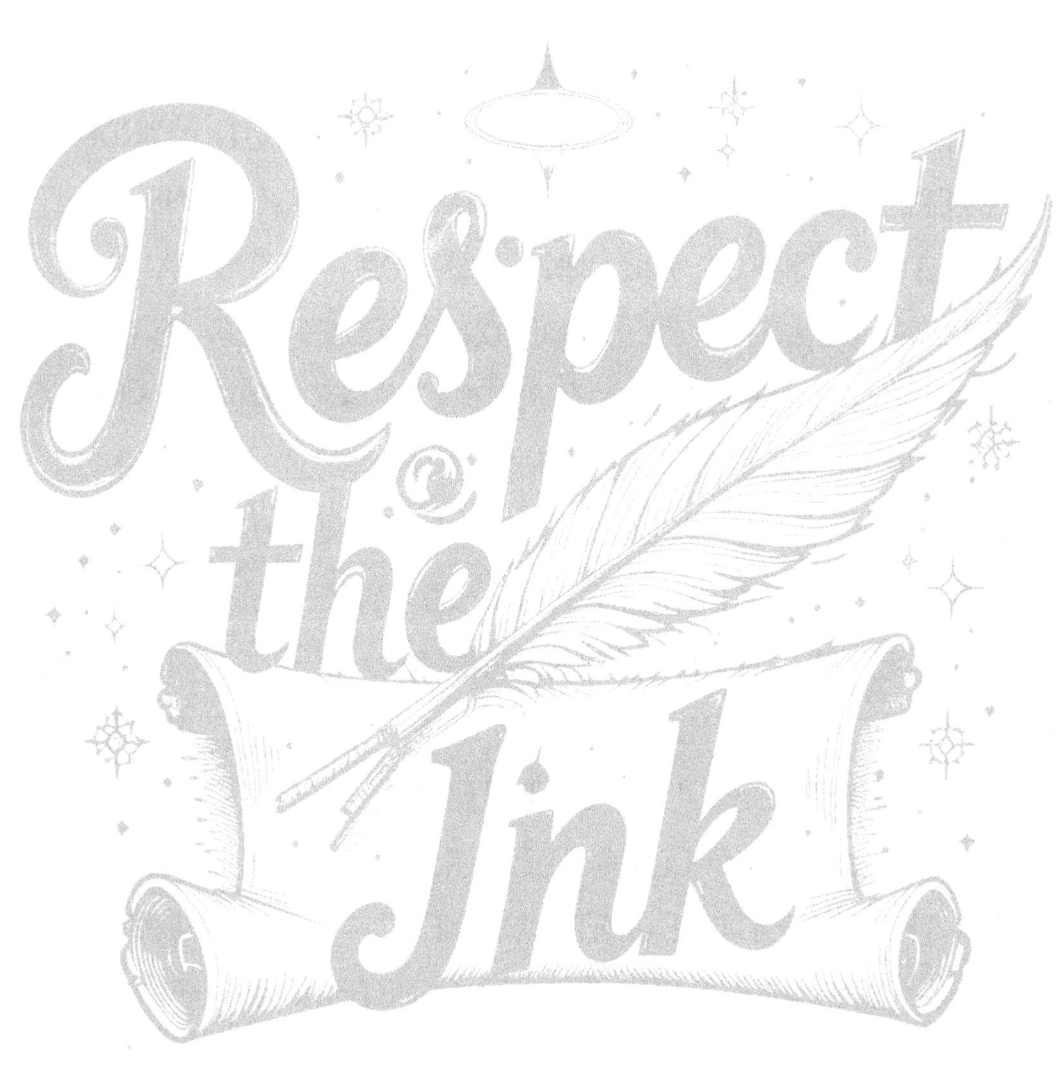

Practice Your Flow

Practice Your Flow

Practice Your Flow

Practice Your Flow

Much love for picking up this book.

If it spoke to you, taught you something, or just felt firme in your hands — I'd be real thankful if you dropped a quick review.

Every word you share helps this small project grow and reach more homies out there who vibe with the culture.

Gracias por tu apoyo